# The Day the World WENT WACKY

By Janine Suter

Illustrated by Richard Gunther

Dedicated to Mom & Dad

Original edition copyright © 2008 by Janine Suter
Master Books® first printing: August 2009

For information write:
Master Books®, P.O. Box 726, Green Forest, AR 72638.

ISBN-13: 978-0-89051-575-4
ISBN-10: 0-89051-575-1
Library of Congress Number: 2009929843

Printed in China

Please visit our website for other great titles: www.masterbooks.net

For information regarding author
interviews, please contact the publicity
department at 1-870-438-5288.

Master Books®
A Division of New Leaf Publishing Group
www.masterbooks.net

A little while back, I was eating my lunch
When I got out an apple and took a big crunch.
The next thing you know, I was in a big chair
With my mouth open wide and my feet in the air.

And just as the dentist put in a huge filling
(My ears were half deaf with the noise of the drilling),
A really hard question came into my brain,
And my really hard question was DID GOD MAKE PAIN?

Then all sorts of crazy thoughts rushed through my mind.
Why was my great Grandma Nellie born blind?
Why did God make great big prickles and sores
And man-eating bears that can walk on all fours?

Why do bad things sometimes happen to me?
(Like the time that my bottom got stung by a bee.)
If God made the world, and He made it all good,
Then why doesn't everything work like it should?

That night at my house, I had had quite enough.
I reached for the Bible to find out some stuff.
I opened the cover to search for a clue,
And there was the answer. I'll tell it to you.

The key to this mystery is found in the past.
The Bible says God made the world really fast.
It took God six days to create earth and space,
And right on day 6 He invented our race.

When the world was brand new, well, nothing went wrong.
The first man and woman were both fit and strong.
They ate and they played. It was all really cool.
Their brains were quite smart, so they didn't need school.

The creatures in Eden were all best of friends,
So Adam did not need to keep them in pens.
Adam and Eve were good friends with them, too,
As they lived in God's wonderful paradise zoo.

And the Lord God Himself often came for a walk.
It was great to be near Him and they loved to talk.
He'd given them fruit from the garden to eat.
Back then nothing died, so they didn't eat meat.

Now, believe it or not, there was only one rule,
Not a whole bunch like they have at my school.
God had said, "This whole garden is yours to share,
But don't eat the fruit from that tree over there."

"That tree over there makes you know bad and good."
It was perfectly plain and they both understood.
'Cause the words Adam heard really stuck in his head:
"Don't eat that fruit or one day you'll be dead."

But one day the woman just happened to meet
A big tricky snake that walked on four feet.
It was really the devil, who told a big lie,
He said, "Eat the fruit, 'cause you won't really die."

"You should eat it all day if you want to be wise.
The fruit from that tree will just open your eyes."
It looked quite delicious, so Eve dug right in.
She gave some to Adam and that started SIN!

Now the fruit that they ate had a really nice taste,
But as they were eating, Eve noticed her waist.
They both said at once, "My body's on show!"
Then ran to get fig leaves and started to sew.

They made the first clothes in the garden right then,
To cover their bodies, just finishing when
God came to the garden as He often did.
Feeling quite guilty, they ran off and hid.

God called out to Adam and asked, "Where are you?"
Adam called back, "I'm not sure what to do.
   We've nothing to wear and we feel a bit rude
      Chatting with you while we're both in the nude."

So God said, "You're naked? How did you find out?
Did you eat from the tree that I warned you about?"
Adam said, "God, it's the fault of my wife!
She gave me the fruit that has started this strife."

The woman said, "I'm not the one you should blame!
That snake over there was in on the game.
He tricked me by saying that you were unfair
For making strict rules for this garden we share."

Now Satan had entered that serpent to trick
Adam's wife, Eve, and it worked pretty quick.
So God cursed him there saying, "Crawl on your belly
Through the dust and the grime and the mud that is smelly."

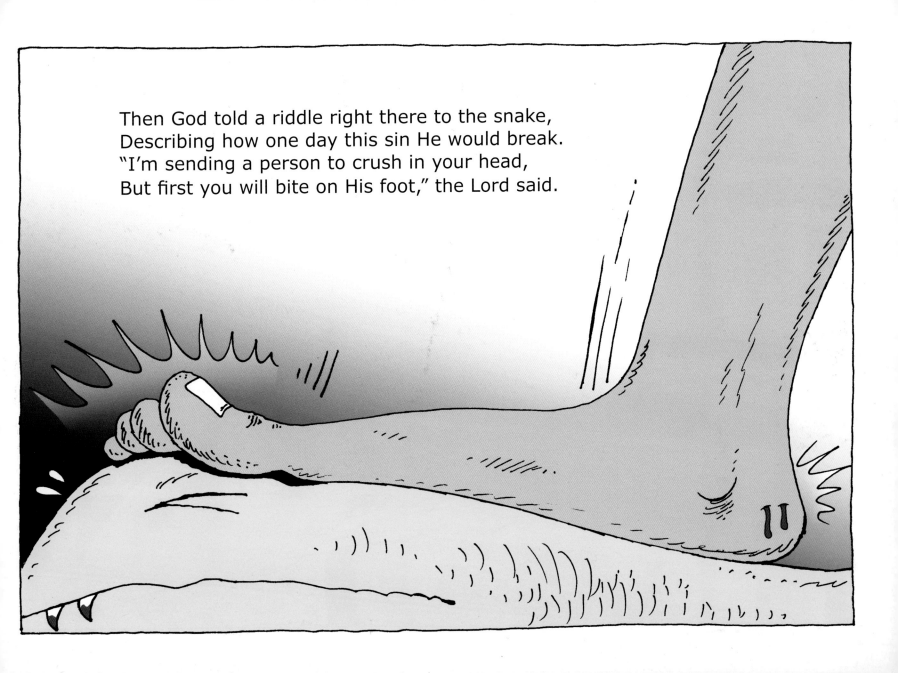

Then God told a riddle right there to the snake,
Describing how one day this sin He would break.
"I'm sending a person to crush in your head,
But first you will bite on His foot," the Lord said.

What this riddle meant was that Jesus would come
To die for our sins 'cause He loves everyone.
Then Eve heard God say, "Sin will make you feel sad
And having your babies will hurt pretty bad."

Next God said to Adam, "Your sin's cursed the ground.
You won't find your breakfast just hanging around.
In future, when you try to grow food from seeds,
You'll sweat and work hard just to fight off the weeds."

"From now on your bodies will start to get sick,
And one day your heart will beat its last tick.
Because of the sin of you and your wife,
One day there will be an end to your life."

God was quite sad 'cause He knew it was true
That now there was something He needed to do. . .
The Lord killed an animal and took off its skin
And then used the blood as a payment for sin.

Then out of that skin and that animal hair
God made the two of them something to wear.
(Animals can't really pay for our sin,
But Jesus' blood can, and this pointed to Him).

Now there in the garden another tree stood —
God's great tree of life with its fruit that was good.
Eating that fruit kept you living forever.
It meant that your body would never die, EVER!

But, if we lived forever in sin we'd be stuck,
Surrounded by sin for eternity. Yuck!
The whole world would just be unendingly bad,
Zillions of years for us all to feel sad.

So God said that Eden was now out of bounds
And to make sure they didn't sneak
   back on the grounds,
A swift flaming sword blocked
   off the way in,
Along with some angels they
   called cherubim.

Well, that day was surely the worst day of all.
It was such a bad day that we call it "The Fall."
We were close to God once, but then sin came along.
It's the cause of all things that we see going wrong.

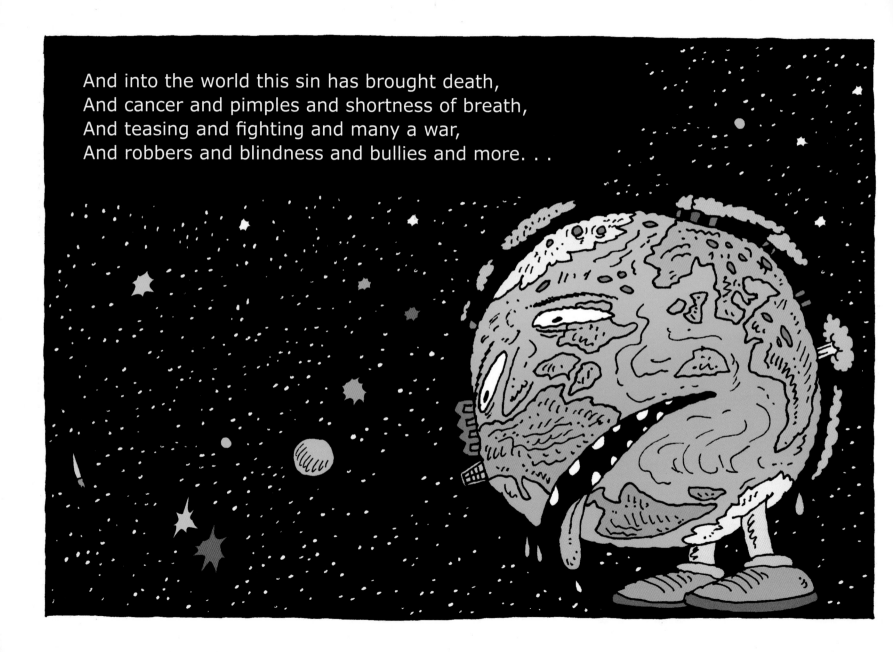

And into the world this sin has brought death,
And cancer and pimples and shortness of breath,
And teasing and fighting and many a war,
And robbers and blindness and bullies and more. . .

You might have thought this has nothing to do
With you or your family, but that isn't true.
Like Adam and Eve, we all want our own way.
It's clear in the Bible we all disobey.

And sin is as vile and as gross as can be.
You're stuck in the stuff and it's in you and me.
That sin in our life means we can't go to heaven
Unless we trust Jesus to have it forgiven.

So next time your molar is giving you pain,
Or your bike gets a flat and you're caught in the rain,
Remember why we're in the mess that we're in —
The world has gone wacky because of this sin.

Now no one can go and see Eden today,
Because Noah's Flood has washed it away.
But God has a plan to make everything new
For all those who love Him.
                    Does that include YOU?

Janine Suter has worked with children professionally and in various ministry roles. This series of books was born out of her desire to present basic theology and apologetics to the next generation. She lives in Melbourne, Australia.

Richard Gunther has illustrated many books for both children and adults, as well as drawing cartoons for a number of newspapers and magazines, and designing a range of educational materials. He lives in Timaru, New Zealand.